CLAN
BUCHANAN

Extensively Revised

COMPILED BY

Alan McNie

CASCADE PUBLISHING COMPANY
Jedburgh, Scotland

4

Genealogical Research:
Research regrettably cannot be undertaken by the publisher. A
non-profit organisation, The Scots Ancestry Research Society,
3 Albany Street, Edinburgh, undertake research for an agreed fee.

ISBN 0 9076140 0 0

Page 1 Explanation:
The illustrated tartan is the modern Buchanan. The motto
on the crest badge means 'Brighter hence the honour'. In
the artist's montage, Clairinch is depicted, an island in
Loch Lomond where the family was first recorded. In the
foreground is the Bilberry, clan plant badge.

Buchanan Country

DETAIL MAP OVERLEAF

The map used below and on the following page is intended basically as a pictorial reference. It is accurate enough, however, to be correlated with a current map. The clan boundaries are only marginally correct. No precise boundaries were kept in early times and territories were fluctuating frequently.

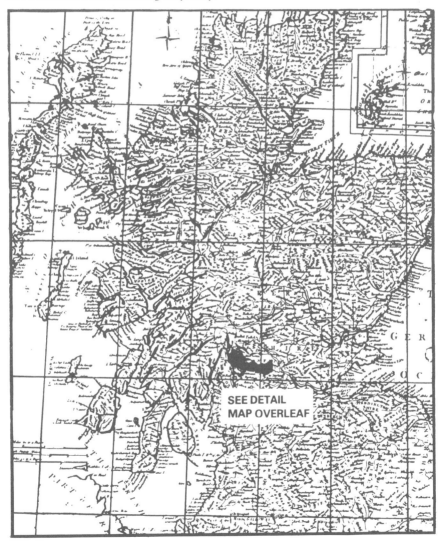

SEE DETAIL
MAP OVERLEAF

Buchanan
CLAN MAP

1. **Arnprior** Important clan branch

2. **Buchanan** Castle Ruins in Parish of Buchanan

3. **Cardross** Distinguished clan branch

4. **Clairinch** Island origin and battle cry (owned by Buchanan Society)

5. **Drymen** Fine gardens at 'Buchanan Arms' Inn

6. **Fintry** Buchanan obelisk at the branch

7. **Killearn** Early clan holding and George Buchanan birthplace

8. **Kippen** Associated with tale of king

9. **Leny** Northerly clan branch

10. **Stirling** Residence of James V

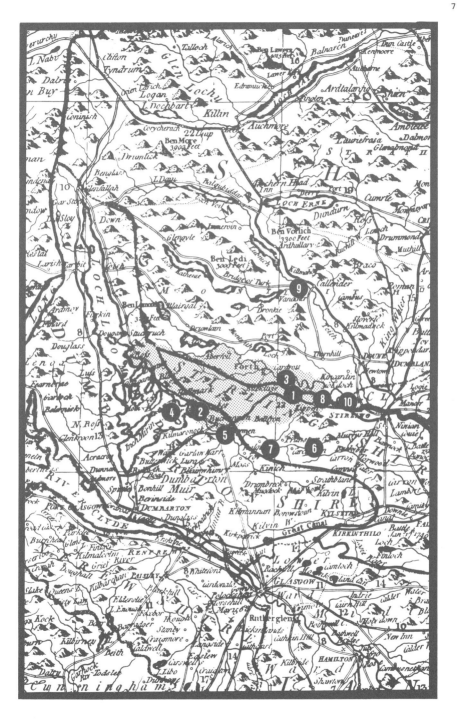

The McIan illustration of Buchanan as published (mid-19th century) in 'The Clans of the Scottish Highlands'

CLAN
BUCHANAN

Condensed from Clans of the Highlands of Scotland
Thomas Smibert, 1850

It is fortunate, that, in the case of the ancient clan of Buchanan, one of its members took the trouble, during the past century, to examine closely into the family archives and traditions, and has left to us a full account of the results of his inquiry. A little allowance being made for family pride and prejudices, the report is a fair one. William Buchanan of Auchmar, the gentleman alluded to, was of a branch of the house nearly connected with the main line of the chiefs. He holds the opinion in his work that the Buchanans are a branch of that great family of the Gall-Gael, otherwise called Gathelians and Argathelians (the latter words being Latinised seemingly, in old documents, from Gael and Oirir-Gael), which we have already mentioned as being traceable to Ireland. Some writers, indeed, say that Gathelian means Gallician or Milesian, but we greatly prefer the explanation above given – that is, that the term Gael created the adjective Gathelian, and not *vice versa*. The words of the author of the history of the Buchanans deserve to be quoted, because they bear on the question of the descent of several clans of the West Highlands, and concur completely with the views expressed on the subject of the origin of the Macdonalds. "I am inclinabale," he says, "to join sentiments with those of the more ancient seneciones (sennachies) or genealogists, who, upon very solid grounds, contend the generality of our clans, and more ancient surnames, whose origin is truly Scottish, to be the real and genuine progeny of the Gathelian or Scottish colonies, which in the several junctures before and afterwards, under the conduct of the two kings, Fergus I and II, came from Ireland, and planted Scotland.'' It may have been observed that, in giving the annals of the great coast-clan of the Macdonalds, two important visitations (at least) of the Irish Celts to Scotland were noticed as of almost certain occurrence, namely, that of the Dalriad-Scots at a very early date, and that of the chief remaining clans of the western isles and coasts about the sixth century. These new immigrants, it was stated, succeeded seemingly to the Dalriad-Scots, when the conquest of the southern Picts drew the main body of that race to the more inland districts, and led, through amalgamations with the Saxon race, to the bestowal of the new name and a new language upon North Britain. Mr Buchanan of Auchmar, it is satisfactory to us to find, coincides in opinion about these two marked and important movements of the Irish Celts to Scotland. He places the arrival of his own clan, indeed, at a later date; but of this we shall speak presently.

The Gaelic name of the house of Buchanan was and is Macauselan. This word is very plainly based on the name of their founder, who, as will be shown, bore the appellation of *Anselan,* so that, but for deference to usage, the term should be set down as Macanselan. The name ultimately adopted, and now borne by them, seems to be intrinsically the same with Buchan, and to be local, or rather to be founded on a word applied to a district of a peculiar description. It is apparently of Saxon, not Gaelic origin. Most probably it has its root in *buck* (in old Saxon *becca* or *bucca*), to which radical may also be assigned many well-known district-appellations over Scotland, as, for example, *Buccleugh (Back-cleugh).* On such a point, however, etymologists may differ without end. The simplest explanation, merely, is given here; and that is, that the word is identical with *Buckholm,* the ''holm of the buck.'' Certain it is, at all events, that the name of Buchanan is admittedly derived from a territory acquired by the ancestor of the family, and still constituting a Dumbartonshire parish of the name; and when it is considered that the territory lay close on the Lowlands, there can be no surprise reasonably felt, either at the Saxonised designation of the locality or its possessors. As the clan were planted, moreover, so long as clans held fixed residences, on and around the slopes of Benlomond, *bucks* must beyond doubt have been plentiful there in the days of old; and this fact goes so far to justify the assigned source of the name. We are aware that the name was of old pronounced, and still is in the pure Scottish dialect, *Buwhannan*. But this fact does not controvert the etymology here preferred.

Anselan O'Kyan, called the Fair, son of O'Kyan, king of South Ulster, was the immediate ancestor, according to Irish and family annalists, of the race of Buchanan. There may be little faith to be put in such accounts at this day, but these are so far confirmed by the Gaelic name, and, besides, where is the better authority to be found? To condemn one manuscript story and adopt another the next moment, has been too unguardedly done even by some of our best authorities on the history of the clans of Scotland. It would be foolish and presumptuous to pretend to be wiser than one's neighbours, but the right way is to endeavour to take a middle course – that is, to follow authentic history where it is procurable, and, where it is not, to view the common tales in the most rational light. The following account of the feats of the first Buchanan who left Ireland, is certainly most suspiciously like the story of Pelopidas the Theban, but it *may* be true, nevertheless. Canute the Dane ruled and reigned in England, and held also part of Ireland, the time being the eleventh century. To celebrate the royal birthday, "Turgesius, the Danish general, sent orders to all the Danish officers in Ireland to repair to Limerick, being their principal garrison and his residence, to assist at the solemnity, fearing nothing that the Irish would or could do in such low circumstances. The general at the same time sent orders to the Irish nobility and gentry, to send to Limerick, against the king's birthday, a thousand, or, as others say, two thousand of the most beautiful of their daughters, to dally with the Danish officers at that festival. Of this the Irish king getting intelligence, resolved to send the desired number of the most clear-complexioned youths that could be found, clothed in women's habit, with long Irish skeins, or daggers, below their clothes, with orders that, so soon as they went to bed with their several paramours, being generally drunk on such occasions, they should stab them with

Loch Lomond *Looking north from Buchanan country*

these concealed daggers, and afterwards seize upon their guard-house, where their arms were laid by, and if matters succeeded, to give a signal by kindling a large fire upon the town wall; the Irish king, with a small party, being absconded in a wood near by, in expectation of the event. These Irish viragoes put their orders in execution to the utmost, and, having given the concerted signal to the king, introduced him and his party to the town, who, without any mercy or resistance, killed all the Danes in the garrison, being destitute of sense, officers, and arms, reserving their general Turgesius for further punishment, which was inflicted upon him by drowning, which then, and as yet, is reputed the most ignominious death among the Irish. Most of all the other Danes throughout the kingdom were shortly after cut off.''

Anselan O'Kyan, son of the Ulster monarch, led the authors of this daring feat, and, when Canute sent a strong force to punish all concerned, the royal youth was compelled, with a party of attendants, to fly to Scotland. So runs the story, at all events. Malcolm II was at the time king of the Scots, and Anselan (otherwise name Absalon, though Anselm may be the true word) was employed by that monarch to act with his followers against the Norsemen of the western coasts. For his good services, he was rewarded with lands of considerable value in the Lennox or Levenax, the tract of country watered by the Leven, on which stream Loch Lomond forms, as it were, a large and deep pool. It is also said that the sovereign took the old way of rendering the task of remuneration more easy, by procuring or facilitating the marriage of Anselan with an heiress of the Dennistoun family. With the noble house which then bore the name and title of Lords of Lennox, and to which the practical service was done rather than to the king, the Macauselans or Buchanans formed early connections, and indeed received from them charters of the main properties which the family of old possessed, and in part still occupy. The first name which occurs in the family story, in authentic charters, is that of Anselan, called Macbeath, from his immediate sire, who obtained the isle of Clare-Inch *(De Clarinis)* on Loch Lomond from the Earl of Lennox, to whom he was Seneschal, about the year 1225. Some time afterwards, the lands of Leckie were granted to the Earl of Lennox, and they are mentioned as lying near to ''Buchanne''. Great part of both properties fell into the possession of the Buchanans, and the last one gave a fixed name to the race. It has been said that the Buchanans were a branch of the Lennox house, but there seems, on the whole, no good reason for discrediting the account which brings them directly from Ireland, whatever one may think of the romantic story of Anselan the Fair, prince of Ulster. The main line of the house was Celtic, almost unquestionably; and there lies the great point in the present argument. The Buchanans, as said, are found from the first as dependents of the house of Lennox, and, however respectable, can scarcely be viewed as kinsmen. They had also a war-cry of their own. "Clare-Inch" was the sound which brought them to the front of the battle. Like the other Irish Celts, they were first gifted with the small islands of the west, and grew strong only through time.

It is in this way, it seems to us, that common sense, at least, should read this and others of the family histories of those remote days. No doubt, the custom of depositing the annals of a clan, with the sennachies (bards or genealogists) was of vast importance in early times, and of which one can now form only an imperfect notion; but yet it is a plan which must ever have been insecure, and the evidence derived from it cannot be held as very conclusive − especially as the parties were expected more to praise their particular chiefs and clans than to record their true deeds. It is necessary, then, to draw, as far as may be, on the colder page of authentic history, in telling the veritable story of each tribe. What could one make out, in the shape of grave narrative, of the career of Fingal, his chiefs, and his compeers, from the fine but shadowy poems of Ossian? Real names may be gathered, but little more. In much the same light must we view the majority of the genealogical records left to us by the family sennachies of the chiefs of the Gael. The "car-borne heroes" must come down to the position of parties mounted on, or drawn by, the galloways and shelties of the west and north-west of Scotland. The nature of the country, its products, and its roads − even if the parallel lines of Glenroy were admitted as genuine pathways of man's making − could never allow of car-driving, any more than the breed of horses would allow of grandeur in the execution of that exercise. The power of the poet is not detracted from, however, but raised by this view of the case. Though we will not here open up the entire Ossianic question, it seems indubitable, that a poet of that name did exist, whose fragments

Macpherson collected more or less extensively, and used with more or less of conscientiousness. But we need to believe no more in the close veracity of the Gaelic bard's pictures than in those of Homer; and certainly it would be somewhat difficult to believe the accounts of the descents of the gods to the plains of Ilion, given by "the blind old man" of Scio.

Gilbert, son of the same Anselan who held the office of seneschal to the Earl of Lennox, was the earliest Macauselan who occasionally received the name of Buchanan; and he assumed it probably from then settling on the special lands of "Buchanne", Clareinch being the older possession. His grandson, Sir Maurice, seems to have been the party who was first fully chartered in the Buchanan lands. He received a *confirmatory* charter of them, at least, from Donald, earl of Lennox; and this deed was assented to by David II in 1369-70. The curious old phrase "carucate" is here used in reference to the territory granted, its signification being nearly the same as "ploughgate". It is not unworthy of note that this Maurice is still named "Macauselan", laird of Buchanan, and the circumstance goes a great way to establish the Gaelic origin of the house. He adhered firmly to the Bruces, however, during their struggles with the Macdougals and other western Celts, and was honoured and rewarded in consequence. The family had by this time attained to very considerable importance, as we find the Laird of Buchanan of the time of Robert II to have been styled by that monarch "our cousin" *(consanguineus noster),* a phrase only used towards men of rank. A marriage contracted with the heiress of Lenny, by John the twelfth laird, added considerably to the property of the house. Sir Alexander, eldest son of John, is said to have accompanied John Stewart, Earl of Buchan, son of the Duke of Albany, to aid the French in their wars with the English. There is good reason to believe that Sir Alexander Buchanan performed on this service a notable personal feat, which mainly gave to the Dauphin of France the victory of Bauge, though the action has been for the most part ascribed jointly to Sir John Swinton, and the Earl of Buchan. The action in question was the slaying, in a hand to hand encounter, of the Duke of Clarence, commander of the English, and brother of Henry V. In the history of the Buchanan achievements, as will be seen from the following extract, there appear solid grounds for adopting this conclusion. Sir

Loch Lomond *Looking south to Buchanan territory in distance on left*

Alexander Buchanan, he says, "meeting the Duke of Clarence, who was very conspicuous upon account of a coronet beset with a great many jewels affixed to his helmet, with his couched spear with the utmost vigour made toward him; the duke in the same posture met his antagonist, upon whose breast-plate the duke's spear slanting, Buchanan pierced at once through his left eye and brain, whereupon he instantly fell from his horse. Buchanan in the meantime getting hold of the coronet, and putting the same upon the point of his spear, cried to his countrymen to take courage, for that there was a token he had killed the English general, which the English noticing, made no further resistance, but committed their safety to their horses' heels, there being killed of them, besides Clarence, twenty-six officers and other persons of quality, and near three thousand soldiers, besides two thousand taken prisoners, with very little loss to the Scots, there being none of account killed upon their side. This victory, as it gave a great check to the affairs of the English, did no less erect the drooping circumstances of the French, of which the dauphin was so sensible, that he created the Earl of Buchan his master of horse, and Wigtoun, high constable of France, and rewarded all the other persons of distinction according to their merits, particularly Buchanan, whom he bountifully rewarded, and for preservation of his heroic achievement, added to his former bearing, a second tressure round the field, flowered and counterflowered, with flower-de-luces of the second, and in a crest, a hand coupee, holding a duke's coronet, with two laurel branches wreathed round the same; which addition was retained by the family of Buchanan in all time thereafter." It is almost impossible to explain the ducal coronet in the arms, unless upon the supposition of this account being correct. The famous *fleurs-de-lis* of the royal French arms might have been granted for general merits, but the ducal coronet cannot be so interpreted. It continued ever afterwards to form a part of the armorial bearings of the Lairds of Buchanan. Sir Alexander, who won for his house this honourable distinction, was soon afterwards killed at Vernoil, AD 1424.

Patrick, fourteenth Laird of Buchanan, made a fortunate marriage with an heiress of the Galbraith family, obtaining thus Killearn and other properties. Here it may not be out of place to remark that the name of Galbraith points out clearly the general character of the permanent occupants of the Western Highlands. It signifies the "brave stranger" and, though that term might apply to a Norse rover, yet it is far more likely, from the position of the Galbraith possessions, that the line was Irish or Gall-Gaelic. The native Gael, it may reasonably be supposed, gave the title to some brave visitant from the Irish shores. The case proves, with that of the Buchanans, that we should not always demand the prefix of "Mac" in a family name, in order to be convinced of its Celtic origin. Similar marriages to that with the Galbraith heiress extended afterwards the power and possessions of the Buchanans, and many cadets branched off from the main stem, whom their sires were enabled to raise to the position of respectable landed gentry. At length the main line came to a close, as regarded male descendants, in the person of John, counted as the twenty-second Laird of Buchanan. He left two daughters – one wedded to Stewart of Ardvoirlich, and the other to Buchanan of Lenny. The death of John Buchanan of Buchanan took place in 1682. Before his decease he had been forced, through pecuniary difficulties, originating partly with his immediate predecessors and partly with himself, to enter upon such transactions for the sale of his estates as ultimately took nearly the whole from his daughters and his race, after a tenure of six hundred years. Buchanan of Auchmar, whose manuscript history was composed at the commencement of last century, states the entries and unbroken possessions of the Lairds of Buchanan, in the Lennox and elsewhere, to have brought a rental of thirty thousand merks. Even if allowance be made for extensive exaggeration, this computation would still show the family to have been among the more wealthy of the landed gentry of Scotland, the value of money at the time being considered. The family of Montrose obtained the greater part of the Buchanan property lying on Loch Lomond. It fell to them by an easy purchase, and Buchanan House, the ancient seat of the chiefs of the name, is now the principal residence of the ducal race of Montrose. Its designation renders it a durable memorial of the ancient lords of the region. But at the death of the last of them, as Auchmar observes, "the flourishing fortune of the family was destroyed, and itself extinguished."

The direct and undeniable offshoots of the house of Buchanan, from its long occupancy of a wealthy and important position, may be expected to have been somewhat numerous. The family historian claims the chieftainship for his own line of Auchmar, but, even in his day, as also long since, the claims of the house of Arnprior have generally received the preference. Into this dispute there is no necessity for here entering. The principal cadets of the line may be given as its annalist gives them, though, if their representatives yet live, the lands which they once owned know them in many instances as lords no more. There were once estated gentlemen of the house, however, bearing the following territorial appellations – "Auchmar, Spittel, Arnprior, Drummakill, Carbeth, Lenny, Auchneiven, and Miltoun," as also "Cashill, Arduill, and Sallochie". From these branches, as well as from the main line, sprung such a multitude of others, if we may trust to their historian, that the Buchanans must be widely spread over Scotland, though holding now very different denominations. From the long continuance of the family, its very considerable possessions, and its many acknowledged cadets, as well as from the principles of nomenclature in old days, we doubt not but that the blood of the Buchanans is really disseminated more widely than mere names would lead one at first to suppose; but it is impossible to assent to the attribution of some hundreds of Highland and Lowland families to the line of Buchanan, upon the traditional evidence which its annalist would have us to accept. It may fairly be allowed that the Macanselans (or Macauselans), of whom various families yet remain in the west of Scotland and in Ireland, were Buchanans; and indeed they at one time claimed the chiefship. The Macmillans, also, seem really to have sprung from an ancient laird of the line, and derived their name, according to the Highland fashion of doing these things, either from their immediate progenitor being "bald", such being the meaning of "Mailan", or from his especial name of Methlan. The Maccolmans spring likewise from the Buchanans. The now Lowland family of Spittal acknowledge the same descent, we believe, though the main ground for doing so is, that one of the Buchanans was a Knight-Hospitaller. However, tradition favours the idea, as also, though less strongly, that the Morrises and Morisons owed their origin to one of the Maurices, lairds of Buchanan. The conjecture is merely given here for the satisfaction of family curiosity, though we own to a belief in the three cases specially noticed.

Stirling Castle

Of course the annals of the admitted cadet-branches of Buchanan can not and need not be detailed here. There is, nevertheless, a memorable story connected with one of the Buchanans of Arnprior, which amusingly illustrates the times in which he lived. The tale has often been told, but, in place of any illustrated version, the simple original is here given: ''John Buchanan of Auchmar and Arnprior was afterwards termed King of Kippen, upon the following account: King James V, a very sociable debonair prince, residing at Stirling, in Buchanan of Arnprior's time, carriers were very frequently passing along the common road, being near Arnprior's house, with necessaries for the use of the king's family, and he having some extraordinary occasion, ordered one of these carriers to leave his load at his house, and he would pay him for it, which the carrier refused to do, telling him he was the king's carrier, and his load for his majesty's use, to which Arnprior seemed to have small regard, compelling the carrier in the end to leave his load, telling him, if King James was king of Scotland he was king of Kippen, so that it was reasonable he should share with his neighbour king in some of these loads, so frequently carried that road. The carrier representing this usage, and telling the story as Arnprior spoke it to some of the king's servants, it came at length to his Majesty's ears, who, shortly thereafter, with a few attendants, came to visit his neighbour king, who was in the meantime at dinner. King James having sent a servant to demand access, was denied the same by a tall fellow, with a battleaxe, who stood porter at the gate, telling there could be no access till dinner was over. This answer not satisfying the king, he sent to demand access a second time, upon which he was desired by the porter to desist, otherwise he would find cause to repent his rudeness. His majesty finding this method would not do, desired the porter to tell his master that the Good-man of Ballangeich desired to speak with the King of Kippen. The porter telling Arnprior so much, he in all humble manner came and received the king, and, having entertained him with much sumptuousness and jollity, became so agreeable to King James that he allowed him to take so much of any provision he found carrying that road as he had occasion for; and, seeing he made the first visit, desired Arnprior in a few days to return him a second at Stirling, which he performed, and continued in very much favour with the king always thereafter, being termed King of Kippen while he lived."

It is also impossible to omit all notice of a clansman of the Buchanan, who would of himself suffice to shed on the name an undying lustre. Of course, reference is made to the historian of Scotland, and her greatest scholar, George Buchanan.

The fate of men of talent and learning in old times was singular enough in many respects, but in nothing so remarkable as in regard of the strange repute which their accomplishments created for them in life, and entailed posthumously upon their memory. Whoever stood eminent above the vulgar in point of acquirements, was popularly set down either as a wizard or as a fool and jester. It was the fortune of Friar Bacon, for example, of Sir Michael Scott, and of Thomas the Rhymer, to be ranked in the former class, while George Buchanan, for two centuries after his death, actually went among the common people of Scotland under the denomination of the "king's fool", and was seriously believed by them to have held that honourable office. Few persons who can remember the flying sheets sold by the hawkers only a quarter of a century ago, will fail to recollect one collection of silly and obscene anecdotes to which the name of George Buchanan was appended. Several reasons may be assigned for the utter ignorance of the true character of this eminent individual – one of the first scholars of his own or any other age – which so long prevailed among the generality of his countrymen. The leading one, however, undoubtedly is, that he composed his works, with trifling exceptions, in the Latin tongue, impelled thereto by the fact of its being the common language of the learned over the whole civilised world, and also by the rude and unformed condition of the vernacular speech of his own land. It is somewhat unfortunate for the fame of Buchanan, that, just as the many have grown more capable of appreciating the productions of his genius in the form in which they appear, the taste for the language of Rome should have fallen into comparative decay.

George Buchanan was born in the year 1506, in the parish of Kellearn, situated in that portion of the ancient district of Lennox which lies in Stirlingshire. The branch from which he sprung was that of Drummakill, of which house his father was second son, his mother being Agnes Heriot, of the family of Trabroun, in East Lothian. In

the old farm-house of Middleowen, on the Blane water, of which some portions yet remain in a newer dwelling, George, the third of five sons, was born. The death of his father threw the family into an embarrassed state, but, by the generous care of a maternal uncle, the future scholar received the elements of a good education at Dumbarton, and was sent subsequently to complete his studies at Paris. Though but fourteen years of age, he soon began to distinguish himself there by his talents for the composition of Latin verses. His uncle died, however, after two years had been spent at the Parisian university, and Buchanan was forced to return home by poverty and ill health. On his recovery he attempted to find a new path to fortune by joining the Duke of Albany's French auxiliaries in the expedition against England in 1523. That campaign proving completely abortive, he resumed his favourite studies in the capacity of a pauper exhibitioner at St Andrews, where he obtained the degree of bachelor of arts. John Mair, a doctor of the Sorbonne, was a leading professor at that time in the Scottish College, but he taught a sophistical logic by no means pleasing to his clear-headed pupil, who accoringly vented on him some juvenile epigrams, not of very great merit though sufficiently severe. For example, when Mair published a book, and prefixed to it a pun on his own Latinised name of "Major", calling himself in the title, with affected modesty, "Major (greater) by cognomen only," Buchanan gave forth the epigram which we here roughly translate. The Cretans, it may be observed, were the most noted liars of antiquity: –

> "When, reading Major (great by name alone),
> You find in all his book no sane page shown,
> Muse not when you the title's truth descry –
> The very Cretans did not always lie."

Returning to France, then the principal seat of polite learning, Buchanan took the degree of master of arts in the Parisian university in 1529, and continued struggling to maintain himself by private teaching till 1531, when he was nominated to a professorship in the college of St Barbe. This was a poor position, however, and he was glad to accept, soon afterwards, the office of tutor to Gilbert Kennedy, Earl of Cassilis, with whom he returned to Scotland in 1537. The principles of the Reformation then formed the great topic of discussion and agitation in the European world, and Buchanan became one of

St. Andrews

John Knox portrait and signature

their most zealous advocates. While John Knox swayed the minds of the common people by his antimonastic invectives in their own homely mother-tongue, Buchanan addressed himself to the more educated classes, and endeavoured to enlighten their minds in reference to the then new doctrines. We know not, indeed, if the part performed by him was not the most important in that age, when so much of the feudal subserviency of the many to the few still characterised the social condition of the countries of Europe. Be this as it may, it was at the request of James V, whose natural son had been placed under his tutorage, that Buchanan produced successive satires on the Romish priesthood, the last of them being "the Franciscan", a piece unequalled for terrible yet truthful severity, as well as perfect Latinity, since the days of Juvenal and Persius. It so unmercifully exposed the general conduct of the monks, that the half-converted king himself could not save the author from the rage of Cardinal Beaton and the clerical brotherhood. He was imprisoned, but contrived to escape to England. Protected in London for a time by Sir John Rainsford, he at last found a better refuge at Bordeaux, Paris being rendered unsafe by the appointment of Cardinal Beaton as ambassador there. At Bordeaux, his now known and proven learning obtained for him the chair of humanity in the new college of Guienne, and he lived there admired and respected for a number of years, though still an object of hostility to the Romish priesthood of Scotland.

Buchanan wrote at this period his two original Latin tragedies of the "Baptist" and "Jephthah", and composed versions besides, in the same tongue, of the "Medea" and "Alcestis" of Euripides. The exquisite scholarship evinced in these productions was not their sole or principal merit. By producing them he accomplished one phase of the Reformation, affecting deeply the instruction of youth in schools. His labours served to banish those *mysteries* which the pupils were wont to enact periodically, and to substitute for them his own sound and healthy dramas. "Jephthah" is a piece full of tender sentiment and passion, while the "Baptist" contains a new and stern denunciation of clerical bigotry and hypocrisy, as well as a regal tyranny.

In 1547 we find Buchanan in Paris, acting as regent in the college of Cardinal le Maire. Here he enjoyed the friendship of the eminent scholars Turnebus and Muretus, as he had before done of the two Scaligers. An invitation to accept the principalship of a new university at Coimbra, in Portugal, seemed to promise the Scottish scholar a higher and stabler position than he had ever yet enjoyed, and he removed thither accordingly. But the death of his main protector at the court of John III exposed him anew to the assaults of the clergy, and, after being catechised, confined, and tormented by them for a year and a half, during which time he composed his beautiful version of the Psalms of David, he was glad to escape to England. From that country he recrossed the channel to France, where he was more secure, and most highly esteemed. For a number of years thereafter he was attached to the family of Marshal de Brissac, whose son's education he superintended, producing at the same time his long philosophical poem "De Sphæra" (upon the universe). When the unfortunate Mary Queen of Scots came to France to wed the Dauphin, the poet wrote their Epithalamium, and, on the return of the prematurely widowed princess to her own country, she seems to have invited him to accompany her as assistant in her classical studies. She subsequently gave to him part of the temporalities of Crossraguel Abbey for his maintenance, to which provision the Earl of Moray added the Principalship of St Leonard's College, St Andrews. Warmly countenanced by Moray, Morton, and the strong party of reformed nobles generally, Buchanan could now publish his collective satires on priestcraft without much fear, though he lost the queen's favour thereby. He also became eminent as a member of the General Assembly, and sat in 1567 as moderator of that body. When Mary fell into dissensions with her subjects, and at last fled to England, Buchanan took the side of the Earl of Moray, and drew up a paper called a "Detection" of the royal doings, for which he has been greatly censured by the defenders of the queen. At a later period, when James VI became ripe for receiving his education, Buchanan was called to the high office of his principal teacher. That he succeeded in imbuing his pupil with an extensive knowledge of letters, is a fact known to all the world, and that he at least did his utmost to keep him free from the faults incidental to his high position, or to which he was constitutionally prone, is also universally admitted. For the special use of James, he wrote his tract "De jure regni", a piece inspired by

Mary, Queen of Scots

noblest spirit of constitutional freedom. But the king preferred the flattering counsels of the under-tutor, Young, to the sound lessons of his head-preceptor, whom, indeed, he latterly hated with a bitter hatred.

The latter years of the life of Buchanan were expended on his "History of Scotland" and here again he spoke what he certainly believed to be the truth respecting Queen Mary. James Melville tells us in his "Diary" that he and others, on seeing the sheets of the work at press, remonstrated with the now aged author on the danger of exciting the king's anger. "Tell me, man," said the historian, "if I have spoken the truth?" "Yes, sir, I think so," was the reply of the party addressed. "Then I will bide his feud, and all his kin's", retorted Buchanan. He was at this time very ill in health, and died about a twelvemonth afterwards on the 28th of September, 1582, at the age of seventy-six. Before that event, King James did attempt to make him retract portions of his history, but he resisted all solicitations of the kind; and he is traditionally said to have been at last so far fretted as to bid the royal agent inform the monarch that no threats could affect him, as "he was going to a place where few kings could come".

The Buchanans of Ardoch, one of the most respectable families of the name, are not mentioned by the historian of the house, and possibly received their direct territorial designation after his day, or form, in his view, a section of some other line mentioned. They claim to belong closely to the main stem of the lairds of Buchanan, and have for a long time held a high position in the Lennox, which lies chiefly in Dumbartonshire, but occupies also a part of the county of Stirling. It was in the section of the Lennox lying in the latter shire that the great scholar, whose name and story have just been mentioned, George Buchanan, was born and brought up. Buchanan of Ardoch was a member of one of the later parliaments of Great Britain, and his house has always been ranked as among the most respectable of those yet bearing the name. The remark has been made, that, of the cadet-branches of Buchanan, several hold their old lands no more. This statement is true; but the Carbeth Buchanans, as well as others, yet possess the lands assigned to them by their forefathers.

Buchanan Associated Names

Associated names have a hazy history. Sometimes they had more than one origin; also clouding the precise location of a particular surname might be that name's proscription or of course a migrant population. Even the spelling of surnames was subject to great variations, shifting from usually Latin or Gaelic and heeding rarely to consistent spelling. In early records there can be several spellings of the same name. Undoubtedly contributing to this inconsistency is the handwriting in official records, which was often open to more than one spelling interpretation.

With regard to the 'Mac' prefix, this was, of course, from the Gaelic meaning, son of. It wasn't long before it was abbreviated to 'Mc' or 'M', until we have reached the position now where there are more 'Mc's' than 'Mac's'.

COLMAN, CALMAN   An early Old Irish name with Latin origins, columba, a dove. A variant, Colman has Scandinavian origins. In 1482 William Colman cleared of part in detaining King James III in Edinburgh Castle. In 1682 Alexander McAlman, dean of Argyll, allowed to take the Test. An ancestor of MacCalman or MacColman (Dove's sons) was called Colman, who was the third son of the 7th chief of Buchanan.

COUSLAND   Origin from nameplace, Cousland, Midlothian, 3½M. ENE Dalkeith. In the 13th century, Patric de Crebarrien (Carberry) was a charter witness. John Cousland was a Stirling resident, 1522. Walter Cousland was a Stirling councillor, 1527.

DONLEAVY, DONLEVY   Some of this name originated from the Buchanans of Drumikill, with the progenitor being Finlay, a son of a Buchanan.

DOW, DOVE   Either from Gaelic dubh (pronounced doo) and meaning black or anglicizing of MacCalman (see Colman). Robert Dow, appears as Perth landholder, 1497. William Dove, resident of Glass (8¼ M west of Huntly), 1716.

GIBB, GIBSON   Son of Gib(b), a shortened form of Gilbert. The Buchanans of Arduill were later called Gilbert (Gilbertson). In 1521 David Gyb was an assize member. Rothesay Castle was surrendered by Johun Gibson in 1335. Glaswegian David Gibsone listed as charter witness, 1451.

GILBERT, GILBERTSON   Either from Old English personal name Gliberht or from Buchanans of Arduill, later called Gilbert. In 1329 John filius Gilbert, bailie of Bute, made a payment. Archie Gilbertsone, in 1482, was declared innocent of detaining James III in Edinburgh Castle.

HARPER This name from the musician, who acted as hereditary official to important families such as Buchanan chieftains. In 1296 William le Harpur rendered homage at Edinburgh, as did Robert le Harpur of Are.

LENNIE, LENNY From lands owned by the Buchanans of Leny (1M NW Callander). John de Lany from 1325-26 was constable of Tarbert. Patrick Lany in 1545 was a witness at Lany.

MACASLAN, MACAUSLAN, MACAUSLAND, MACAUSLANE This name and its variants have a Buchanan association, but merely a territorial one, as they had their own clan identity, originating with an early chief, Anselan. Absalon or Absalone, between 1208-14 witnessed a gift of the church of Campsie (1½M NW Lennoxtown) and during the same period witnessed gift of another church this time in Cardross (3½M NW Dumbarton).

MACCALMAN (See Colman)

MACGIBBON Son of Gibbon. Sometimes Gibeon written for Gilbert (see GILBERT), hence its possible Buchanan association. Donald McAne Gibsoun lived in Tiree, 1541. Duncan M'Gibbon in 1706 was a fencible man in Glenlyon of the Duke of Atholl.

MACKINLAY, MACKINLEY From the Gaelic form of Finlayson, son of Finlay. A Buchanan branch was the Mackinlay Buchanans. Gillaspyk M'Kynlay acted as witness concerning Craignish, in 1493. John M'Ynla in 1561 attested a bond of manrent in Glenurquhart.

RISK, RUSK From Gaelic riasg, a morass with sedge. Originating apparently with the Risks of Drymen, who became a cadet of Drumnikill, and consequently associated with the Buchanans. John Reisk in 1552 was a Glasgow witness. Rusk, a common name in Strathearn, is probably a variant of Risk.

Some Clan Notables

Buchanan, James *(1791-1868)* Born in Lancaster, Pennsylvania, this fifteenth president of the United States was a son of Scots-Irish immigrants. His Democratic presidential term coincided with one of the most turbulent periods in American history. The slavery issue, a failed policy of Centra American control and a severe depression were among major issues that made his presidential term extremely difficult.

Buchanan, Isaac *(1810-1882)* This Glaswegian emigrant, following a Scottish education, soon became a successful Canadian businessman, establishing a commercial firm in Montreal, Toronto and Hamilton. Politically active, he helped suppress the Papineau Rebellion of 1837. He held a seat in the Executive Council of the federal government and is often described as the real father of 'National Policy'.

Buchanan, John *(1819-1898)* Born and educated in Scotland, this pioneering botanist left for work in New Zealand where he pursued a lifelong interest in botany. He published a volume on the indigenous grasses of his adopted country and was a founder of the New Zealand Institute.

Buchanan, Benjamin *(1821?-1912)* This talented Glaswegian became a successful financier and industrialist at an early age with interests in rail, shipping and food. A skilled and patient negotiator he was called to arbitrate between his partners at one time and on another occasion, when retired, a union dispute.

Buchanan, David *(1823-1890)* This Edinburgh native, with an Australian law degree became a stormy politician and critic, who immersed himself in Australian issues. As a legislative member he became obsessed with divorce reform but other reform measures also interested him.

Buchanan, John *(1844-1925)* A Glaswegian graduate, who became a world-renowned scientist. His oceanographic studies were carried out in the most meticulous scientific manner. His numerous widely accepted and innovative theories involved the physical and chemical properties of seawater and the seacoast.

MR. MᶜKEAN BUCHANAN AS MACBETH.

MAC: To be thus is nothing:
But to be safely thus:— Our fears in Banquo
Stick deep, and in his royalty of nature
Reigns that, which would be feard.

MACBETH   Act 3. Sc 1.